Helping plants grow well

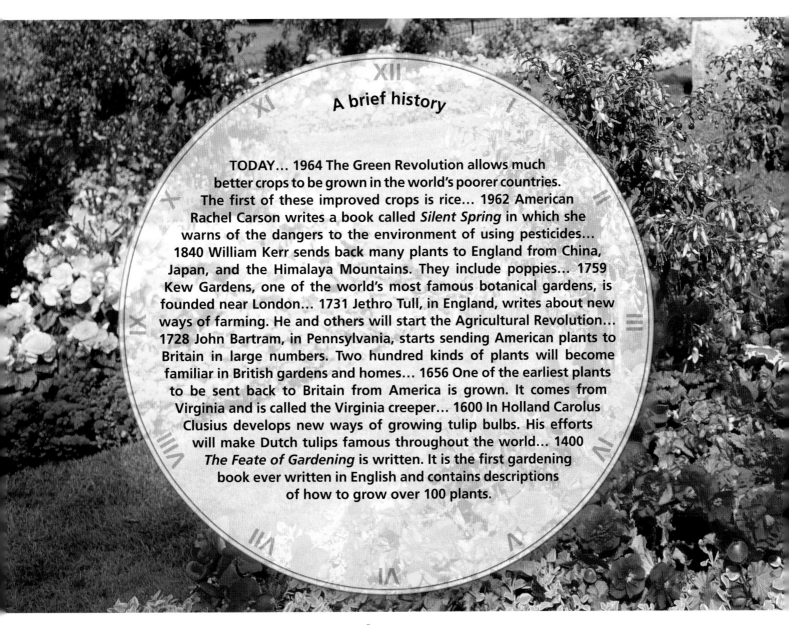

A brief history

TODAY... 1964 The Green Revolution allows much better crops to be grown in the world's poorer countries. The first of these improved crops is rice... 1962 American Rachel Carson writes a book called *Silent Spring* in which she warns of the dangers to the environment of using pesticides... 1840 William Kerr sends back many plants to England from China, Japan, and the Himalaya Mountains. They include poppies... 1759 Kew Gardens, one of the world's most famous botanical gardens, is founded near London... 1731 Jethro Tull, in England, writes about new ways of farming. He and others will start the Agricultural Revolution... 1728 John Bartram, in Pennsylvania, starts sending American plants to Britain in large numbers. Two hundred kinds of plants will become familiar in British gardens and homes... 1656 One of the earliest plants to be sent back to Britain from America is grown. It comes from Virginia and is called the Virginia creeper... 1600 In Holland Carolus Clusius develops new ways of growing tulip bulbs. His efforts will make Dutch tulips famous throughout the world... 1400 *The Feate of Gardening* is written. It is the first gardening book ever written in English and contains descriptions of how to grow over 100 plants.

Dr. Brian Knapp

Word list

These are some science words that you should look out for as you go through the book. They are shown using CAPITAL letters.

BRANCH
A part of the stem of a plant that grows sideways, and that carries leaves and flowers.

CEREAL CROP
A crop, such as wheat or rice, grown for its seeds.

CROP
A plant that is grown for food.

DISEASE
An illness caused by invisible microbes in the air.

ENERGY
The power that is used to keep living things alive.

FERTILIZER
Chemicals used as plant food to help plants grow.

FLOWER
The part of the plant that is designed to make new plants. Most flowers are made up of delicate petals.

FRUIT
The part of the plant that contains the seeds. Apples and oranges are fruit.

HEALTHY
In good condition, free from illness or injury.

HUMUS
The rotted remains of dead plants. It is the fine, black material on the surface of many soils.

LEAF, LEAVES
Green sheetlike parts of the plant that are designed to catch sunlight.

MICROBE
A tiny creature that is carried in the air, and that can cause disease.

NOURISHMENT/ NUTRIENTS
The food that a plant needs.

POTBOUND
A plant that has grown too many roots for the pot it is in.

ROOT
The part of the plant below the ground.

SAP
The watery liquid that travels through plants in special tubes in the roots, stems, and leaves.

SEED
The part of a plant that can make a new plant. Seeds are generally hard. Some are very large, but others can be very small.

SHOOT
The growing part of the plant above ground.

SOIL
The mixture of tiny pieces of rock and rotting plant material in which plants grow.

STEM
The main, upright part of the shoot. Branches grow off from the main stem.

VEGETABLE
A crop grown for the food in its leaves, stems, and roots.

WATERLOGGED
A soil that is filled with water. Roots need air as well as water, but a waterlogged soil has no air and so is bad for most plants.

WILTING
When leaves go limp because the plant cannot get enough water from the soil.

Contents

How does a plant grow?

People sometimes have difficulty keeping plants at home because they do not understand all of the plant's needs.

Some people are said to have "green thumbs," meaning that they are good at keeping their plants **HEALTHY** (Picture 1). Other people never seem to be able to get anything to grow.

You only have to look at the plants in people's gardens to find out that some people are better at growing plants than others. Farmers, of course, cannot afford to take chances with how well their plants will grow and have to make sure they get it right every year.

So why are plants so difficult to grow?

The parts of a plant

We can learn a lot about what a plant needs simply by looking at it (Picture 2).

Plants are made of two parts—the part above the ground and the part below the ground.

The part above the ground is made of **STEMS** and **BRANCHES**. On the branches are **LEAVES**, **FLOWERS**, and **FRUIT**. Plants use their leaves to take in air and sunlight and make food. The flowers and fruit are used to make **SEEDS**, which will produce new plants.

The part below the ground is the **ROOT**. All plants have roots, and most plants have a network of roots that branch out many times. The roots stretch out into the **SOIL** around the plant to gather water and **NOURISHMENT** for the plant.

If we can see how plants manage to grow, then we might be better able to see how we can help our own plants grow better. That is what we will do in the next pages.

(Picture 1) Plants are living things, just as we are living things. You know that we need the right kind of food and water to keep us healthy, so we can expect that plants also have special needs. This means that simply watering a plant will not meet all of its needs.

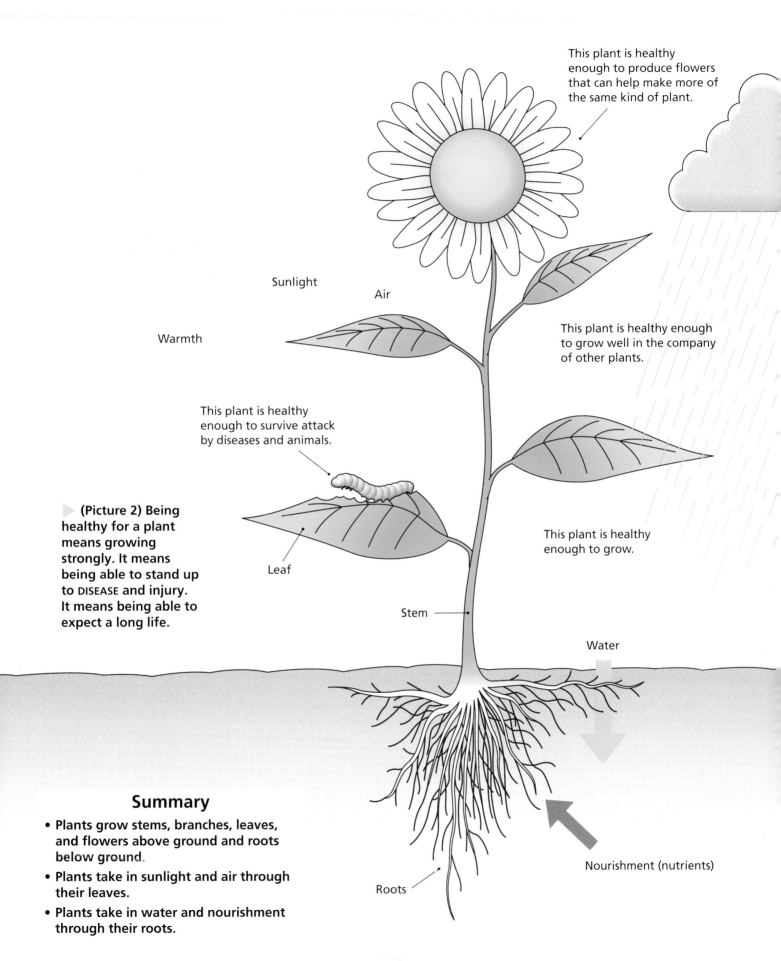

This plant is healthy enough to produce flowers that can help make more of the same kind of plant.

Sunlight

Air

Warmth

This plant is healthy enough to grow well in the company of other plants.

This plant is healthy enough to survive attack by diseases and animals.

▶ (Picture 2) Being healthy for a plant means growing strongly. It means being able to stand up to DISEASE and injury. It means being able to expect a long life.

This plant is healthy enough to grow.

Leaf

Stem

Water

Nourishment (nutrients)

Roots

Summary

- Plants grow stems, branches, leaves, and flowers above ground and roots below ground.
- Plants take in sunlight and air through their leaves.
- Plants take in water and nourishment through their roots.

Water

Plant roots collect water and air from the soil. They suffer if there is too little water or too much water.

Plants are filled with water. If you crush a leaf or a stem in your hand, the water comes out as a pale green liquid we call **SAP**.

Water is what gives plants shape. Plants suck up water from the soil and use it to pump up their leaves. They also get nourishment from the water, as we will see later in this book.

▼ **(Picture 1) When a plant wilts, its leaves become limp and hang from drooping branches. Finally, the leaves lose their green color, turn brown, and begin to shrivel up.**

Plants can recover from the early stages of wilting, but not once the leaves have started to shrivel. That is why, if plants are to grow well, they need to be watered regularly.

Wilting

Without water a plant cannot grow quickly. As soon as a plant runs out of water, it simply stops growing.

Many plants lose water all of the time through their leaves. So they need a new supply to replace what they lose.

Plants get their water from the soil. If they cannot get enough water to replace what they have lost, then their leaves will soon go limp. This is called **WILTING** (Pictures 1 and 2).

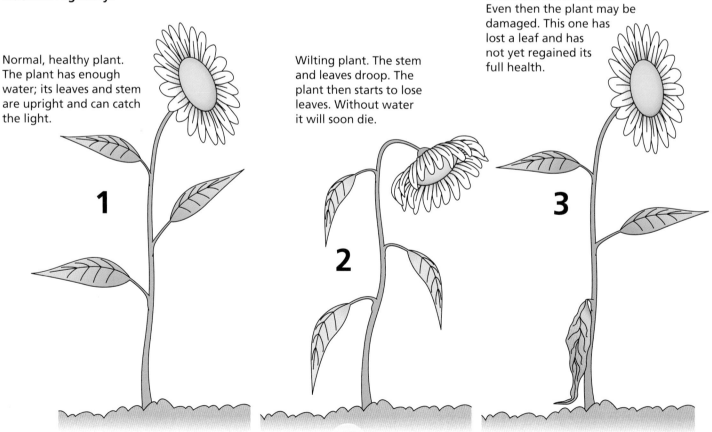

Normal, healthy plant. The plant has enough water; its leaves and stem are upright and can catch the light.

Wilting plant. The stem and leaves droop. The plant then starts to lose leaves. Without water it will soon die.

If the wilting plant is watered in time, it can be saved. Even then the plant may be damaged. This one has lost a leaf and has not yet regained its full health.

1

2

3

(Picture 2) Notice the lower leaves have wilted more than the upper leaves. The lower leaves have probably wilted too far to recover.

Dried out

Many plants grow in places where the soil dries up regularly. When this happens, these plants simply stop growing. A cactus is one type of plant that is adapted to live in dry soil and to go long periods without water (Picture 3).

Wilting happens most commonly with garden and houseplants. That is because the plants we grow often come from parts of the world that have no drought, and so they are not used to coping with it.

Waterlogging

You might think that because plants need water all of the time, they would grow well if stood in water. Some do. All the plants that live in swamps, marshes, rivers, and ponds, for example, grow well in water. Rice is an example of a swamp plant. But plant roots also need air, and most plants cannot get air in a **WATERLOGGED** soil. That is why many plants stop growing if the soil becomes waterlogged.

Plants that are waterlogged for a long time will eventually die. That is why most plants will only grow well in a well-drained, moist, not soggy soil.

▼ (Picture 3) These cactus plants will not wilt. They are ideal for a desert garden.

Summary

- Plants need a supply of water to keep their shape.
- When plants have too little water, they stop growing.
- When soils become very dry, some plants wilt.
- Many plants die if the soil becomes waterlogged.

Nourishment

Plant roots grow down to get liquid food from the soil.

Plants make their own food from the world around them. They make the food in their leaves. One important source of **NOURISHMENT** is the soil the plant is growing in (Picture 1).

The problem for a plant is how to get the nourishment from the soil to their leaves. The way they do that is to suck up the nourishment in the water found in damp soil.

We can't easily see roots sucking water and nourishment from the soil, but we can see how they move through the plant by using colored water and a celery plant (Pictures 2 and 3). We use celery because it has big water-carrying pipes that are easy to see.

Where the nourishment comes from

Most of the nourishment a plant needs comes from the rotting of dead plants on the soil surface. This rotted material is called **HUMUS**.

▼ **(Picture 1) Look carefully at some soil, and you will see masses of tiny roots reaching out to get moisture and nourishment.**

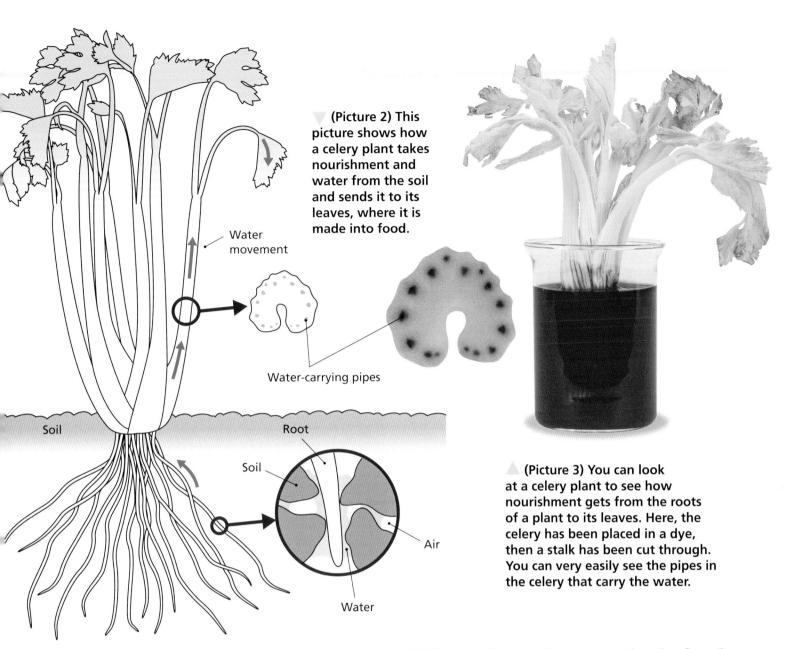

(Picture 2) This picture shows how a celery plant takes nourishment and water from the soil and sends it to its leaves, where it is made into food.

Water movement

Water-carrying pipes

Soil

Root

Soil

Air

Water

(Picture 3) You can look at a celery plant to see how nourishment gets from the roots of a plant to its leaves. Here, the celery has been placed in a dye, then a stalk has been cut through. You can very easily see the pipes in the celery that carry the water.

Gardeners make humus by rotting down their old plants. They do this in a special pile called a compost pile. If you get some well-rotted garden compost from the bottom of a pile and squeeze it, liquid plant food will come dripping out. It's just what the plants need.

Pot plants are not given this kind of nourishment because people don't want smelly compost in their homes. That is why they feed them with liquid food. It is called **FERTILIZER**.

When plants have too little food

If plants do not get enough food, they grow slowly or poorly. They may look weak and stunted. If just one part of their food is missing, they may not produce good fruit, their flowers may be small, or their leaves may turn a funny color. When plants are weak, they are more likely to get a **DISEASE**.

Summary
• Nourishment comes from the soil.
• A natural source of nourishment is called humus.
• A source of liquid nourishment is called fertilizer.

Light

Plants use light to make food for growth. Plants grow poorly in too little light, but some are also damaged by too much light.

Plants use sunlight to make food. The secret of how they do this is the green substance in leaves (Picture 1). It is what makes plants green. The green substance works like a chemical factory, using light to change air, water, and nourishment into food.

Most of the green substance that soaks up sunlight is found in leaves, but there is some in green stems, too.

Plants move to the light

If you watched many plants, you would see their leaves and flowers turn to keep facing the Sun throughout the day. In fact, plants don't just move each day to keep facing the Sun, they also grow taller to get the amount of sunlight they need (Pictures 2 and 3).

▼ **(Picture 1) A leaf draws water and nourishment from the soil through tubes in its stem. Inside the leaf air, water, and nourishment are combined to make food using energy from sunlight.**

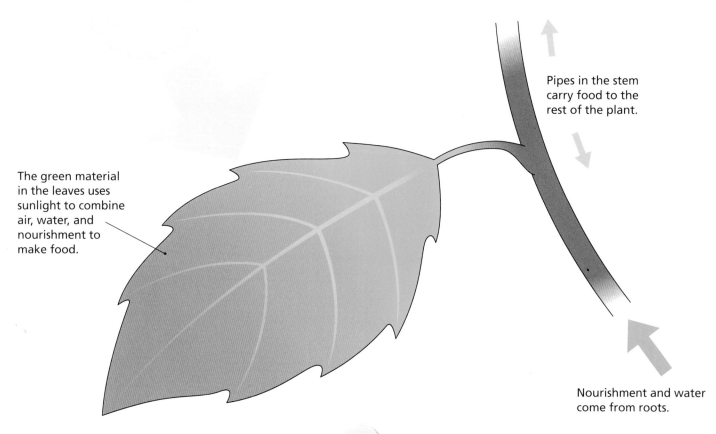

Pipes in the stem carry food to the rest of the plant.

The green material in the leaves uses sunlight to combine air, water, and nourishment to make food.

Nourishment and water come from roots.

(Picture 2) Tree leaves spread out to capture light.

(Picture 3) Some plants, such as ferns, need only a little light. If these plants were put in full sunshine, their leaves would become scorched, and the plant would die.

(Picture 4) In this experiment seeds were put on damp tissue paper in two containers on a windowsill. When the tissue paper dried out, it was dampened again.

The lid of one container was always left on, while the lid of the other container was left off. In both cases the seeds started growing, but only those that found light turned green.

Leaves use light

A plant cannot grow unless it has enough food, and it cannot make enough food unless it can get enough sunlight. This is most important when seeds first burst into life (Picture 4).

New **SHOOTS** have some reserves of **ENERGY** in their seeds. If you put a seed in a dark place and let it sprout, you will find that its stem is thin, and its leaves are tiny. Both leaves and stems are white. The green substance that gives them color only develops when there is light. Unless light is found, the green substance never develops, and the plant cannot make new food. Within days the spindly, white seedling will run out of energy and die.

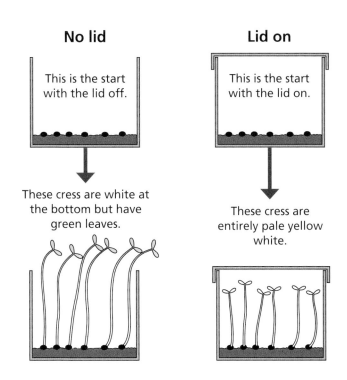

No lid

This is the start with the lid off.

These cress are white at the bottom but have green leaves.

Lid on

This is the start with the lid on.

These cress are entirely pale yellow white.

Summary

- Plants need light to make food.
- Food is made by the green substance in the leaves.

11

Warmth

Plants are very sensitive to warmth. But each type of plant needs just the right amount of warmth, so plants can be harmed by both too much cold and too much warmth.

A plant will only grow in temperatures that suit it. In parts of the world where there are cold winters, the coolness of autumn causes many plants to stop growing and shed their leaves. They then rest through the winter until the warmth of spring triggers them into growth again. Warmth controls the growing season.

▼ (Picture 1) In harsh conditions plants can become covered in frost and ice. They will kill many leaves.

Frost

Frost is often a plant killer (Pictures 1 and 2). If the water in plants freezes, it turns to ice and swells. That can burst the leaves apart. You do not notice this during a frost because the plant is frozen solid; but when the plant thaws out, its leaves turn black and die. You will see many garden bedding plants turn black after frosts in autumn.

Growing temperatures

Every plant has its own range of temperatures—when it will start growing, when it will grow best, and when it will stop growing because it is too hot or too cold (Picture 3). For example, wheat that grows naturally in cool parts of the world will grow if the temperature is above freezing. It grows fastest when its leaves

◀ (Picture 2) You can give plants a warmer and more frost-free environment by putting them in a greenhouse. In this way they will start to grow sooner in the year.

Spring

Summer

Winter

Autumn

warm up to 25°C. That is why it grows best at the start of summer. But it stops growing completely when the leaves get hotter than 31°C. That is why wheat will not grow in places where it regularly gets very hot, for example, near the equator.

Some other plants, such as pineapples, need warm conditions throughout the year. That is why pineapples will not grow in cool climates.

▲ (Picture 3) Changes in temperature have dramatic effects on many plants, causing them to shed leaves and stop growing in autumn, to grow new leaves in spring, and to flower in summer.

Summary
- Plants need warmth to grow.
- Frost kills many plants.
- Some plants will not grow if it gets too hot.

Giving plants enough space

If plants are crowded together, they will not be able to get enough sunlight or enough nourishment and water from the soil.

Seeds grow where they fall or where they are planted. They cannot move around like animals. So if they grow too close together, they will not have enough space to grow properly.

Tall and spindly

A plant needs to grow leaves, or it will not be able to soak up the light it needs to make food. So a plant that is growing in crowded conditions will have to spend energy trying to grow upward to reach above its neighbors.

The chances are it will not have enough energy left to grow large leaves

▲ (Picture 1) Here are some trees growing together. They have been planted close together so they will grow tall and straight and have few branches. Trees are grown like this to make their trunks easier to use, but we would not grow pot plants like this because they would seem too spindly.

after spending so much effort growing a tall stem (Picture 1).

A plant that has more room to grow will start to grow many leaves before it grows a tall stem. In this way the leaves can make enough food to grow a sturdy stem, many branches, and even more leaves (Picture 2).

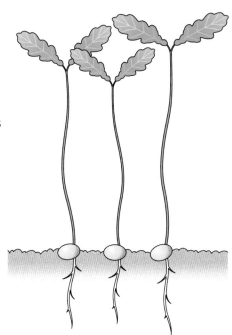

(Picture 2) The plants on the left are growing with lots of space all around. The plants on the right are growing tightly packed together. All of the plants are the same age. Notice that the plants on the left have bigger roots than the ones on the right.

Potbound

If you grow a plant in a pot, it can spread its leaves, but it cannot spread its roots. Plants like this grow up well until the pot is almost choked with roots. When roots curl around the outside of the soil, the plant is called **POTBOUND** (Picture 3). Until a plant becomes potbound, it will grow well; but as soon as it becomes potbound, it will grow only very slowly. That is because the plant will have taken all of the nourishment it can from the soil in the pot, and the roots will have no chance to spread out and look for more. A plant like this will need to be repotted.

Bonsai trees are kept small by having their roots clipped regularly.

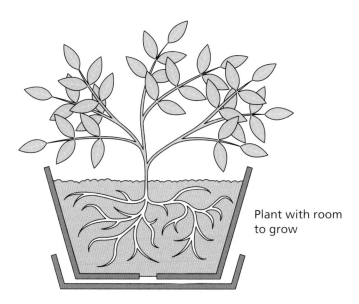

Plant with room to grow

Potbound

(Picture 3) When a plant is potbound, the roots grow around and around in the pot. Sometimes they come out of the drainage hole in the bottom of the pot and even run across the surface of the soil.

Summary

- Plants need enough space to grow good leaves.
- Plants need to have enough space to grow as much as they need.

Pests and diseases

Plants are food for many animals, including tiny creatures called microbes. They can keep plants from growing well.

You will remember that plants are food for all other living things (Picture 1). When we grow plants and eat them, we call it farming and gardening. When other animals eat our farm or garden plants, we call them pests. Tiny creatures called **MICROBES** can get into plants and cause **DISEASE**.

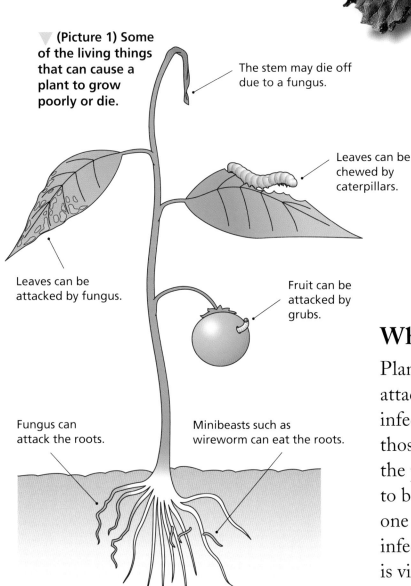

▼ **(Picture 1) Some of the living things that can cause a plant to grow poorly or die.**

The stem may die off due to a fungus.

Leaves can be chewed by caterpillars.

Leaves can be attacked by fungus.

Fruit can be attacked by grubs.

Fungus can attack the roots.

Minibeasts such as wireworm can eat the roots.

▲ **(Picture 2) Common diseases of plants are called mildew and rust. They develop fastest in damp conditions, which is why a warm, wet summer brings on more disease than a dry one. This leaf has rust. It is causing the dark-colored blotches.**

Which plants get disease?

Plants have natural defenses to stop attack by disease. All plants can become infected by microbes (Picture 2), but those that are not growing well will have the poorest defenses and are most likely to be affected. Once a plant is affected by one disease, the chances are it will soon be infected by other diseases. That is why it is vital to try to treat any disease quickly.

(Picture 3) This caterpillar is rapidly munching its way through the leaves of a tree.

Cultivated plants (the ones we use for food or for our gardens) have been bred to grow quickly, but they are usually less able to fight diseases. Cultivated plants are also grown together in large numbers, so it is easy for a disease to spread quickly between plants.

Which plants are attacked by pests?

We grow plants because they are a concentrated source of food. All animals know this as well, and so plants are eaten by a wide range of wildlife (Pictures 3 and 4).

Most destructive are insects, mainly because they occur in larger numbers than any other living thing on Earth. They are also difficult to stop. A fence, for example, will keep out grazing animals like sheep, but it will not stop greenfly and other insects. In general, they have to be attacked by spraying plants with insecticides (Picture 5).

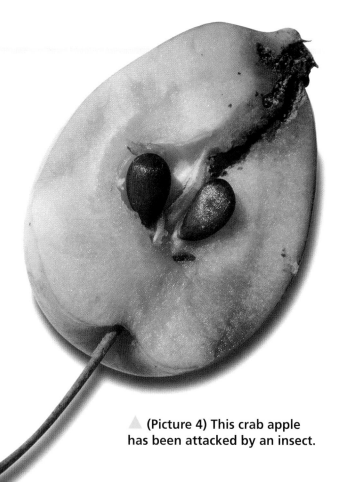

(Picture 4) This crab apple has been attacked by an insect.

(Picture 5) One way to deal with pests and diseases is to spray plants with chemicals.

Summary

- Microbes can cause disease.
- Insects that eat the plants we want to grow are called pests.
- Both microbes and pests can kill plants.

Why we need plants to grow well

Plants are an important source of food for people. That is why we need to make sure that our food plants grow well.

As you now know, plants can make the food they need from the world around them. But people cannot do that, so they must eat either plants or animals.

Although there are hundreds of thousands of kinds of plants in the world, we can only get food from a very small number. That is why we have to make special efforts to grow the plants we can eat. We call these plants **CROPS** (Picture 1).

Cereals

A plant stores most of its nourishment in its seeds and sometimes in its roots. So farmers grow many plants for their seeds.

All of the seed-producing plants, such as wheat, barley (Picture 2), rice, and corn (maize) are relatives of wild grasses. They are called **CEREAL CROPS**. Half of the world's people depend on rice; most of the rest depend on wheat and corn.

▼ **(Picture 2) A field of barley.**

(a)

◄▼ **(Picture 1) (a) This is a natural forest. In it are a few wild plants that we can eat. But this land will not provide food for many people.**

(b) This is farmland. The wild crops that we cannot eat have been cut down, and the wild crops we can eat have been bred to be stronger and give more food. This land will provide food for many people.

(b)

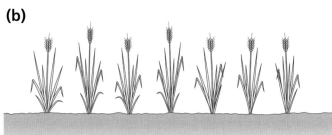

(Picture 3) Pumpkins are a traditional autumn dish. They are a vegetable crop.

Fruit and vegetables

A few plants store nourishment in their leaves or stems, or underground in swollen roots called tubers. Cabbage, carrots, turnips, sugar beet, pumpkins (Picture 3), and potatoes are some of them. They are called **VEGETABLES**.

We eat a range of **FRUITS** because they contain special nutrients that we need to stay healthy. Some fruits, like apples and mangoes, grow high in trees, while others, like strawberries and bananas, grow on plants closer to the ground.

Pasture

We keep many animals to provide milk, eggs, and meat. All of these animals have to eat too. So we also grow grass and cereals to feed animals. Grassland for animals to eat is called pasture.

Farmland

The places where food crops are grown, both for people and animals, are called farmland.

Farmers have to make sure that weeds do not grow in the fields where crops are planted. They must also protect crops from pests or being damaged by disease. This task takes up much of the farmer's time throughout the year.

Summary

- Growing plants is vital for our lives.
- The plants we can eat are called crops.
- Farms are places where food crops are grown.

Plants around the world

Plants are successful at growing in different conditions around the world.

If you were to take a journey from the icy wastes of the North Pole to the hot rainy lands near the equator, you would see many different kinds of plant.

Different conditions suit different kinds of plant, as you can see in Picture 1. Near the North Pole it is always cold—often freezing, sometimes snowy. Near the equator it is warm, and rain falls all year long.

In each place you would find plants that can get everything they need to grow well from the place where they grow. But if you took one of these plants and put it in a different part of the world, the chances are that it would die.

Summary

- Different plants grow well in different parts of the world.
- Plants that grow well in one part of the world may not succeed in other parts.

(Picture 1) Each part of the world has its own kinds of plants that grow well.

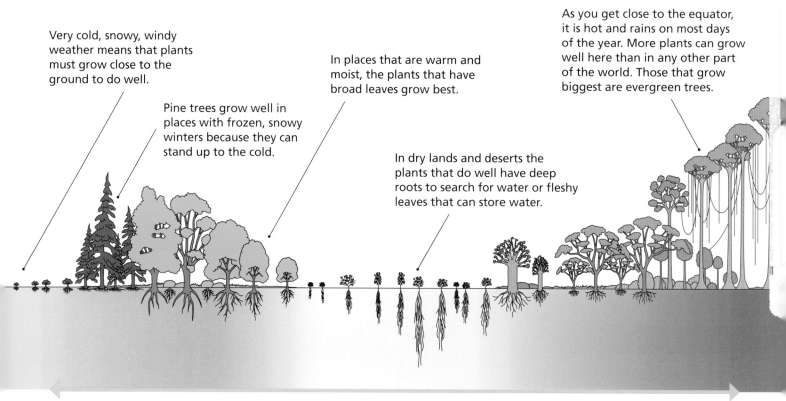

Very cold, snowy, windy weather means that plants must grow close to the ground to do well.

Pine trees grow well in places with frozen, snowy winters because they can stand up to the cold.

In places that are warm and moist, the plants that have broad leaves grow best.

In dry lands and deserts the plants that do well have deep roots to search for water or fleshy leaves that can store water.

As you get close to the equator, it is hot and rains on most days of the year. More plants can grow well here than in any other part of the world. Those that grow biggest are evergreen trees.

To the North Pole

Equator

Alpines grow on mountains and in icy wastes. They grow close to the ground on poor, rocky soil.

Heathers grow on moorlands where the soil is damp and cool.

Look carefully at this picture. If you look up the trunk of the tropical palm tree, you will see a Swiss cheese plant! Its roots grow down in search of nourishment.

Bromeliads are tropical plants that live on rocks or in trees. They use their roots less than most plants and instead take nourishment from water that falls in the center of their leaves.

Cacti grow in deserts, where it is hot, and the rainfall is unreliable.

Can you be too kind to a houseplant?

Plants need the correct amount of sunlight, water, warmth and nourishment. You can kill them with "kindness."

You can make the mistake of thinking that houseplants are garden plants in a pot and try to water and feed them just like the ones outside. Very often that will cause problems. That is because conditions indoors are very different from those outside. For example, there is much less light indoors, and the air is much drier.

Most of our houseplants do not grow naturally in this country (Picture 1). People have searched all over the world to find plants that we can keep at home. So the instructions that come with the plant tell you how to keep conditions as close as possible to what the plants are used to (Picture 2).

Plants that keep best indoors

Which plants do you think are the easiest to keep in a room that always has dry air, gets hot in the day and cold at night, and where there is not much light? The answer is plants from parts of the world that are naturally like this.

Some plants, such as bromeliads, orchids, and Swiss cheese plants, can grow out of the soil on the branches of giant rain-forest trees.

Some plants, such as begonias and ferns, grow on the forest floor in deep shade.

Ferns are plants that grow well in the shade. They get enough light from shady conditions and do not need too much sunshine. If these plants are put in the sunshine, their leaves will burn and turn brown.

◄▲► (Picture 1) Some houseplants, such as this begonia (right) and fern (above), come from tropical forests (left). These plants need shade, so putting them on a windowsill in full sunlight may kill them.

(Picture 2) You can see when you get things wrong because the plant will not grow well. If the air is too dry, for example, the plant's leaves will get brown tips. If you give a plant too much water, its stem will rot. The pictures on this page are examples of common houseplants and the conditions they like best.

Spider plant

Direct sunlight (desert plants thrive, shade plants wilt)

Cyclamen (mountain plant)

Bromeliad (rainforest plant)

A cactus is a desert plant. It is used to growing in a place where there is lots of sunshine but where rain is rare. It is also used to getting every last bit of moisture from the soil. If you think they would grow better by being given more moisture, then you would be wrong. If you keep a cactus in wet soil, it will have too much moisture, and it will start to rot.

Plants that are hard to keep

Which plants would be hardest to keep? Those from places where the air needs to be moist all of the time, such as plants from near the equator. They may look great in a garden center, but you have to be prepared to look after them every day.

Many of the common houseplants are bred from plants that come from drier parts of the world, and that grow in the shade. These kinds of plant will live well in centrally heated homes if they are watered just once a week. The spider plant is a common example.

Summary
- Every plant needs to be given the conditions it grows best in.
- Treating indoor plants as though they were garden plants can often result in disaster.

Index

Science Matters!

Grolier Educational

First published in the United States in 2003 by Grolier Educational, Sherman Turnpike, Danbury, CT 06816

Copyright © 2003
Atlantic Europe Publishing Company Ltd.

All rights reserved. No part of this publication may be reproduced, stored in a retrieval system, or transmitted in any form or by any means— electronic, mechanical, photocopying, recording, or otherwise—without prior permission of the publisher.

This product is manufactured from sustainable managed forests. For every tree cut down at least one more is planted.

Author
Brian Knapp, BSc, PhD

Educational Consultant
Peter Riley, BSc, C Biol, MI Biol, PGCE

Art Director
Duncan McCrae, BSc

Senior Designer
Adele Humphries, BA, PGCE

Editor
Lisa Magloff, BA

Illustrations
David Woodroffe

Designed and produced by
Earthscape Editions

Reproduced in Malaysia by
Global Color

Printed in Hong Kong by
Wing King Tong Company Ltd

Picture credits
All photographs are from the Earthscape Editions photolibrary.

Library of Congress Cataloging-in-Publication Data
Knapp, Dr. Brian J.
    Science Matters! / [Dr. Brian J. Knapp].
        p. cm.
    Includes index.
    Summary: Presents information on a wide variety of topics in basic biology, chemistry, and physics.
    Contents: v. 1. Food, teeth, and eating—v. 2. Helping plants grow well—v. 3. Properties of materials—v. 4. Rocks and soils—v. 5. Springs and magnets—v. 6. Light and shadows—v. 7. Moving and growing—v. 8. Habitats—v. 9. Keeping warm and cool—v. 10. Solids and liquids—v. 11. Friction—v. 12. Simple electricity—v. 13. Keeping healthy—v. 14. Life cycles—v. 15. Gases around us—v. 16. Changing from solids to liquids to gases—v. 17. Earth and beyond—v. 18. Changing sounds—v. 19. Adapting and surviving—v. 20. Microbes—v. 21. Dissolving—v. 22. Changing materials—v. 23. Forces in action—v. 24. How we see things—v. 25. Changing circuits.
    ISBN 0-7172-5834-3 (set)—ISBN 0-7172-5835-1 (v. 1)—ISBN 0-7172-5836-X (v. 2)—ISBN 0-7172-5837-8 (v. 3)—ISBN 0-7172-5838-6 (v. 4)—ISBN 0-7172-5839-4 (v. 5)—ISBN 0-7172-5840-8 (v. 6)—ISBN 0-7172-5841-6 (v. 7)—ISBN 0-7172-5842-4 (v. 8)—ISBN 0-7172-5843-2 (v. 9)—ISBN 0-7172-5844-0 (v. 10)—ISBN 0-7172-5845-9 (v. 11)—ISBN 0-7172-5846-7 (v. 12)—ISBN 0-7172-5847-5 (v. 13)—ISBN 0-7172-5848-3 (v. 14)—ISBN 0-7172-5849-1 (v. 15)—ISBN 0-7172-5850-5 (v. 16)—ISBN 0-7172-5851-3 (v. 17)—ISBN 0-7172-5852-1 (v. 18)—ISBN 0-7172-5853-X (v. 19)—ISBN 0-7172-5854-8 (v. 20)—ISBN 0-7172-5855-6 (v. 21)—ISBN 0-7172-5856-4 (v. 22)—ISBN 0-7172-5857-2 (v. 23)—ISBN 0-7172-5858-0 (v. 24)—ISBN 0-7172-5859-9 (v. 25)
    1. Science—Juvenile literature. [1. Science.] I. Title.

Q163.K48 2002
500—dc21
                                            2002017302